Herenow

selected poems

by

Fahredin B. Shehu

inner child press, ltd.

Credits

Author
Fahredin B. Shehu

Editor
hülya n. yılmaz, Ph.D.

Cover Design
Fahredin Shehu & William S. Peters Sr.

inner child press, ltd.

General Information

HERENOW

Fahredin B. Shehu

1st Edition: 2018

This Publishing is protected under Copyright Law as a "Collection". All rights for all submissions are retained by the Individual Author and or Artist. No part of this Publishing may be Reproduced, Transferred in any manner without the prior **WRITTEN CONSENT** of the "Material Owner" or its Representative Inner Child Press. Any such violation infringes upon the Creative and Intellectual Property of the Owner pursuant to International and Federal Copyright Law. Any queries pertaining to this "Collection" should be addressed to Publisher of Record.

Publisher Information
1st Edition: Inner Child Press
intouch@innerchildpress.com
www.innerchildpress.com

This Collection is protected under U.S. and International Copyright Laws

Copyright © 2018: Fahredin Shehu

ISBN-13: 978-1-970020-67-0 (inner child press, ltd.)

$ 14.95

Dedication

For my daughter, Tamara

and

my son, Reis

the delights of my Soul

~ * ~

to be aware of the

No-Place and No-Face,

and to love!

Table of Contents

Preface xi
Foreword ~ Editor's Notes xiii

The Abyss of a Surface 3

Down to the Garden 5
The Pilgrims of Love's Temple 6
Slides from the Past 8
Who Was Crazy, and, Who Was Stupid? 10
Sobriety 11
Beneath the Icy Desert 12
While You Meander on … 13
A Gentle Mortification 15
Layers of Fog 17
The Bees of Aleppo 18
Let There Be Word! 19
Moments of Bliss 20
We Knew Not the Separation 21
Toward Hope 22
If I could, ... 23

Two Measures for a Single Soul 25

The Bride 27
The Gift 28

Table of Contents ... *continued*

My Time, Their Burden	29
No-Place	31
The Dark Wind of the Universe	32
A Return	33
Encumbrance	34
Beyond the Calendar-Fast	35
When the Night Arrives ...	36
A Turquoise Ink for Spiritual Letters	37
Amid the Urban Desert	28

Faces from No-Land — 39

That Strange Something ...	41
The Turret	43
My Borough	44
The Abyss of a Surface	45
The Coffin of a Female Corpse	47
Uncle	48
My Fateful White Maltese	49
My Father	50
A Love-Path to Immortality	51
An Emerald Dane	52
I ...	53
HE, Who Is Busy with Love ...	54
Listen, O Life!	55

Table of Contents... *continued*

Faces from No-Place	56

The Weight of Pain   57

I.	59
II.	60
III.	61
IV.	62
V.	63
VI.	64
VII.	65
VIII.	66
IX.	67
X.	68
XI.	69

Innocent Acts of Consciousness   71

So Be It!	73
After the Flood	74
A Years-Collector	76
My Grandmother	78
I Fear Not!	79
The Blooming Acacia	80
The Mirror	81

Table of Contents . . . *continued*

Come on!	82
A Drop of Happiness	83
On Sound, Secrets, Love and Travesty	84
A Love-Song	86
That Wine . . .	87

Epilogue 89

About the Author	91
Contributions to Anthologies, Yearbooks & Journals	95
What Others Are Saying . . .	99
A Few Words from the Publisher	105

Preface

Sonoric Cures

There were sonoric cures we used to call "the medicines for the body and the soul. A kind of Silly Apocrypha, considered by some sages and well-preserved by Sufis of this region. Perhaps, they were handed down from the Chaldean heritage. God knows. It was war-time in Kosovo. We were accustomed with the acoustic contamination from the fighter-jets. I was reading Atma Puja Upanisadas by Osho; the craziest book for the most absurd times in order to escape madness.

I wanted to be a cat for the first time in my life, since I could not walk around freely while cats were copulating by the wall of my aunt where I took refuge. Alicia Bernal was constantly calling me from The Philippines to migrate there. She wanted to rescue an artist.

About 17 months passed after the time when Alicia got out of her bathtub, her left foot slipped on the shiny porcelain floor, and she hit her head, spilling blood all around her.

She whispered, "Kyrie Eleyson". The kind of death I have been longing to face for ages! What a loss for people from all continents whom she embraced for years! She was planning my flight for Christmas this year. A few years after she sent me a Gold Medal for Poetry as the Bridge to Nations. My happiness had reached the clouds upon hearing her intent. Reason and Woman always comprised my Goddess. She was my trinity.

Fahredin Shehu

Foreword ~ Editor's Notes

When a writing by a non-English native author is of the caliber that is exceptional in its exquisite versatility, an editor faces a challenging task: To maintain the integrity of textual complexity while situating the mechanical aspects of language into the authentic authorial voice. Fahredin Shehu is a courageously visionary writer of passionate dedication to any subject of universal relevance he takes upon himself. He is acutely aware of and knowledgeable in lyrical symbolism, the Islamic as well as Christian spiritual and mythological traditions, and linguistic heritages. Shehu does, however, not merely display his keen awareness and knowledge through his written art when his individual poetic objects are concerned but rather enriches the long-established perimeters of poetry as a genre at large. Where, when and to what extent, then, does an editor join in?

Fahredin Shehu is a writer who does not shy away from adopting a modernist approach for his lyrical compositions. Regardless of the name or the fame of an author, such tendency is too often misunderstood. The lack of punctuation, capitalization, a missing rhyme scheme, etc. but also the use of non-Western referents in any given verse are largely viewed by those in the field as "a mistake". *HERENOW* displays a considerable number of poems in which the author does not allow such potential critique to standardize his writings. He does not deviate from his creativity. In fact, he is masterfully attuned to it. In sum: He eloquently and confidently assumes poetic license.

It may be safely argued though that poetic license should not obscure important content. The entire work of a writer who is not a native of an English language-environment can easily be mistaken as being flawed, if that work's content is not adjusted to fit into the broad context of the philological target. And, it is herein where the editor's work comes in. *HERENOW*, thus, has only been subjected to minor changes in language use and to selected application of the traditional form in order to represent itself for what it originally was: An outstanding literary creation.

hülya n. yılmaz, Ph.D.

Liberal Arts Professor, retired from Penn State
Director of Editing Services and Co-Chair,
Inner Child Press International

Herenow

selected poems

by

Fahredin Shehu

Fahredin Shehu

The Abyss

of a

Surface

Fahredin Shehu

HERENOW

Down to the Garden

On a falling rainbow-wing, Seraph waits
for a bruise to turn yellow, down the garden
Arrabal extracts juice out
of the clitoris. Seven by seven years, all cells
as Nacre, are blown by the wind. We used
Aspergillum on the graphene-weft
to reproduce Bosch – all in vein
They copulated when the Moon was
at the 29th Mansion, far from Earth's gravity,
and gave birth to Lithopedion
cleaned their nostrils with the monthlies
Dried pomegranate-peel is far more bitter than
Mandrake juice and Peyote's Mescaline
I stood amidst blood and sonoric pollution
with a bedazzling glare, and I felt
a real sinful, mundane and ignorant
praising scavenge from a rolling stone

Fahredin Shehu

The Pilgrims of Love's Temple

Timeless we remain as those in times
      when Time was adored as God.

There is no morality in the Cosmos
nor mercy when Destiny puts
      a guillotine above your neck.

In a breeze, we flew in flocks.
Far distances, we travelled at half-a-breath.
Horizon and nadir,
East and West had no points.

Our navels, nurtured with sandalwood oil;
Our faces, washed with ozone;
Our hair, anointed with nard;
Our feet, bathed in milk and balm.

With wings, stretched like an eagle's,
With the eyes of the curious, we asked
      a myriad of questions.
We pealed layers of ignorance.
We left a transparent being to get
      burned by the rays of the Sun.

We broke all stone idols to throw
      stones at our hearts.

HERENOW

We walked on the emerald
    on dew-decorated grass,
        akin to pearls from the depth of the ocean.
We wore kelp dresses to cover
Our firm torso – firmer than turquoise
    and amethyst gems.
        One more beautiful than the other!

All of a sudden, we realized what
    we were not.

We understood that we were mere
    pilgrims of Love's temple.
    And, we remained silent.

Fahredin Shehu

Slides from the Past

Moistening her fingers with her lips
She was curling the threads in the days of old
Into scarves and shawls and socks
For us all before the nights began to freeze
The house-walls and ice
Released crystalline sounds
In the middle of the dark room
With a single candle-light
When the strong winter-wind
Brought snow and locked our door
We cried out loud. None of us
Claimed to stay any longer
Falling asleep in a warm room
On dream's wings, we flew
Like a flock of migratory birds
Far beyond the images we saw back home
Or on the black and white TV
I have read the sage writing about
His passage through Heaven and Hell
But he remained alive to terrify us
With his story. Others in the region
Were saying, we shall read him
After five decades – when our hair
Turned grey and our skin got
Wrinkled and pealing like
Grilled aubergines
A city fool started his barking
Better than a real dog

HERENOW

He knew . . . he knew that a light breath
And a warm home make the entire world
He knew not that the world is round
And there is no East and West
He screamed loud when the thunder
Tore the sky apart
I was foolishly looking for a better world
As the one who is ill
Treading the green that is his cure

Fahredin Shehu

Who Was Crazy, and, Who Was Stupid?

The day turned dark
All rainbows dispersed
Everything became fairy tale-like
A tale that none can tell
But to me it was an image
Of Yerevan – a picture brought
By a poet friend who went
To search for the cure
But his son died and he
Wrote a book
By that time, I just tormented myself
With Beelzebub tales
And all know that Gurdjieff
Was not stupid nor crazy

Sobriety

As it was never sufficient . . .

Ducks in the pond
opposite to a garden, a gurgling
river taking away old memories
Those mere things we used to leave
Behind, like the kernels of peaches
we threw behind our backs
while enjoying the juicy flesh without any peels
Dark was the night, it later became starry
They were waiting for the eclipse of the Moon
A few waves of an earthquake shook
the ground beneath our feet
The Solar System showed its sobriety
We played like fools with our fate

As it was not enough like it was never
Sufficient, an eye-opening moment

Fahredin Shehu

Beneath the Icy Desert

Some limbs fell asleep,
dormant as fossils of the Ice Age,
waiting a blue flame of Love
to once again ignite the passion for
another half-life;
full of zest for the Age of Turmoil
when the White Man encroached a soil
and shook the frozen waters, unable to flow
amidst the core of the Earth.

We have been there . . .
assembled to parliament as cantankerous
without finding any truth-particle beneath the Icy Desert.
No ears of understanding were able to hear
the tweets of children with one eye, blue and another, red.
And the hissing blinks of eyes of the curious, rapidly
damaging the vision for the crystalline Truth,
the naked bare, the naked creature.

I heard echoes of distant earths echoing your name
and the winds as wings blowing the grayed hair of mine.
I felt a flock of angels flutter over. Only, they have no
resemblance to them. Or, our Spirit has no measure
for the Love that we never kindled in our hearts. They were
never a figment of it.

HERENOW

While You Meander on the Grey Side of Shade

Opaque feelings, once again, overwhelm
the rusty appearance of her beauty.
        She is at large.

Despite it all, the mean daggers of hate,
a second before the attack, claim:
"When the beauty turns to be a bully
nothing but despair spreads
as a dangerous radiation."

While you, dear,
meander on the grey side of your shade,
myriads of creatures have been born. In
a cyclic motion, they mature to await death
        in long, far too long queues.

From where I stand observing,
there is a shiny Moon, and I see no borders
there on Earth, where the malice sowed
fear and the glutton swallowed
        all dreams and hopes.

The colors of your skins are giving
a powerful glow to the specter
when negative particles
        oscillate the orbits.

Fahredin Shehu

When the awaken amidst you has a parlor
of a gushing river, let me see your
sparkling teeth as beautiful as a pearl. Your veins
      bear the essence of cilantro.

Let me see your progeny rise and prosper
and the product of your hands serve, apart
      from your you-alikes.

Oh human, how beautiful you are and
proud as a peacock! Yielding flocks,
you encroach Goodness and compete in . . .
When you come up here,
you shall see what you have lost in vain.
Only here, you will swear in Time and
      only here, your soul bears no shade.

HERENOW

A Gentle Mortification

Piles of Men-bones and then . . . digging, from the holes hidden deep under earth.
Stones and ashes with sweat of slaves . . . you would think we don't have them today.

My hair turned grey and the vision, blurred. It was suffocated by bizarre images, created throughout the world and beyond. Whoever said and whoever had ever promised us to come down on earth and enjoy our vacation for life demands more than I may see, more than I may feel, more than I may utter the first word of the first language
that of Silence.

There is another Soul evaporating on the deck, and at the shore, the breeze blows, odors of their
smelly sweat. They watch as they wait in the queue their turn to the entrance of death. That Gate open-heartedly awaits so many . . . a way too many
guests for their retirement. There is a vast Space beyond the blissful Knowing and the bells ring beneath the roof of the utmost Heaven.

You see. Even Death is different, not only Fate, not only Joy, not only the uninterrupted Smile,
the one that demolishes every hatred. Even Love is different in the process of your gentle mortification.

Fahredin Shehu

Ask me then, where is Freedom, where is the turquoise bone of Destiny and where are the days as cheap minerals overwhelming Life, taken as corn seeds by the chickens and a rooster with the chirping voice who calls them and does not allow them to have even a grain.

And . . . the flowers are frozen from the snow at April's end. This Spring has betrayed us all . . . sour are the strawberries. You would think you are eating cherries.

And . . . what else do you think we shall do when the Sun burns your shadow until it disappears?

Who said you have a right to call me Life, when in reality I am only a Gentle Mortification.

HERENOW

Layers of Fog

That time is gone
when I would count all layers of fog
just before I entered the dark forest.

A gushing river took all my sins
and the smell of decayed oak-leaves
      filled my chest.

Mushrooms . . . oh, those surprises of a greedy boy!
The dew, falling from the leaves of lianas, the smell
of moss and the cracking boughs
      beneath my feet were scary.

That time is gone
when I would count the stars, and
with each count, a wart appeared on my left hand.

The dark night – a deafening silence,
took all my words and the smell of Ozone, like
garlic, fainted me.

Moon . . . o, that eternal inspiration for
a lustful Man and the mildness of the air
      distilling in my torso, the smell of
      resin and rosemary beneath my nostrils
      pulsating as heart . . .

Fahredin Shehu

The Bees of Aleppo

From the grape pollen, I took
a golden shine. With its wings, I was fondling
nectar lumps as children of his neighborhood
cleans with their sleeves a slobbered nose.

Night, when it dawns slowly, dew
moistening the grass above the tombs . . .
Who knows how to die and
shall resurrect with an illuminated face or
look the Evil straight in the eye?

We loved every child, and the tears, we
collected in wedding-earring-boxes
of suffering mothers. Tears dried
as the nacre of the Ocean. Green
garments, tunics from algae that
brought a Baltic amber to the shores where
we recall our childhood, and crying from
the bruises in our elbows and sweat as buttons
in our foreheads, we sobered up under the shade
of the Oleander when the fragrance
of rosemary, enveloped and covered
the breeze and the winds
heavy with iodine.

A hive there is extinguished, just as
the three-thousand years old city of Aleppo.

Let There Be Word!

Let there be Word!
For in an emptiness only
Gaps of distance are created
For Men and Angel alike.

Let there be a Word of Love!
For we lack it as desert.
      Hot summers need rain.

Let there be a Word
As the scent of a desert flower
In the vastness of a frozen Ocean!
For we lack it.
      A sick one lacks a cure.

Let there be Peace
and Peace alone!
For we lack it.
      A Soulless Merchant lacks a Soul.

Fahredin Shehu

Moments of Bliss

This is a time for my reflection
and I hear the distant thoughts
thinking of killing other Men
thinking of the melting ice of Antarctica
doings of evil against the Pure and the Humble
dying children at our time of age, amid our awe

Rise, oh Man, in revolt
before the Smog of Death fills your chest
and leaves no space for a breeze
for the ozone odor to dispel all the dirt!

Say a word, oh Poet, the Word
as rocket to hit the hearts made of stone
to dismantle the Machinery of Hatred
for a moment and for eternity more
so that we can call out a Moment of Bliss.

HERENOW

We Knew Not the Separation

Statured amid the dew of petty things, returned refreshed
        with lungs full of Myrtle and Pine fragrance,
seeking serenity in a grotesque trammeling of
        worn–out Spirits, I roam, jostling fears
and hopes and forgetting the brand-linen I ought
        to wear – the only thing to be buried with . . .
and the linen written all-over with Saffron and Rosewater
        all of my poems I was unable to write on
friendship for the poet's sensitive Soul who once lived
        in the Constellation of Peace – the same I want to
re-build here, and the bright stars which fell upon
        the wombs of our mothers shall bear witness.

One day, when from the bleach-white, or rather neon-light
skeleton of mine, the shine shall emit the rays from the sky-
wide dome.

Again, I shall return from the mossy ruins where I was
seeking the Beauteousness of your being, and you will
remember the wine we drunk even before
we knew not the separation. And there was none . . . when
the souls of ours merged long time ago
and for eternity and a day more.

Fahredin Shehu

Toward Hope

Walking on the gold beneath our feet
in this damn land we grew up; doomed
orange halogens, on two sides of the street
leading us toward unknown paths of defeat

Toward hope and the tunnel of death
Toward light and all colors of breath

For life is short but we are yet to live
and the stars we watch below
when man is unable to perceive
us mere. And, our glare and our glare

Toward hope and the tunnel of death
Toward light and all colors of breath

We flew over in the starry sky
we asked man and angel why
we ran mad and full of lust
for life. The life is short yet. We
don't trust anymore
anymore
anymore

Toward hope and the tunnel of death
Toward light and all colors of breath
Toward light and all colors of breath
Toward light and all colors of breath

HERENOW

If I could, . . .

If I could only draw my image on your Soul
I'll do it entirely, I'll do it for all

If I could only settle for anything
but the best . . .
Oh no,
don't settle for anything
but for the best!
Oh no,
don't settle for anything
less but for the best!

If the Moon refuses to appear
and the night is as dark as ink in its sheer . . .

If I could only draw you near . . .
yes, draw you near

Since
I don't settle for anything less but for the best
I don't settle for anything less but for the best
I don't settle for anything less but for the best

Fahredin Shehu

Two Measures for a Single Soul

Fahredin Shehu

The Bride

Look at the celebration and the clergy
on that very day in the dusty street, spoiled
children with neon-color
> in their nostrils, balloons of blubs
> in front and behind her, they threw petals
> of red roses and rice

Beside the front-gate inside the yard, there was
a house. A spring had, for ages, stopped to give
water or to refresh the Marigold flowers
and the cobblestone in a blossoming garden

She walked lightly with the right and
then with the left foot, whereas from the eyes
of a mother-in-law, the reflection of an outburst
of the spring has been seen and the jet of
muddy water, which woke up
after many decades

Fahredin Shehu

The Gift

We feared the village barber
more than any demon
from the tales of our grandmothers

I was circumcised in my seventh age
without my consent. That very moment
when the first cyclus of my body cells
jumped out, I realized on my twenty-seventh . . .

Then, I deliberately quit
celebrating birthdays. On my thirty-third, I got
a present: A birthday party, an abstract painting
of our sculptor. That was exactly seven years
after the war. In fact, after two attempts on my life

If they had anyone left to kill . . .

My Time, Their Burden

I followed the sound of that day
Few hours after dawn. They took me
To the far forest to feel the cracks
Of boughs. And my feet slipped
On those decayed leaves

I heard the ripple
A spring
As if I wanted to obey
My thirst for the moment
To extend my life
Or what remained from it

Sure, the dowry
Is every moment
In the breathtaking ozone
With the smell of garlic
And the breath-releasing waves
From a borrowed life
From afar, where there is Angel
Who congruently bears my name

I persisted and extended
The night. Solely, without
An ounce of fear, since it was taken
Long ago already
By the ghosts of all colors

Fahredin Shehu

It seems to me that I am
On the twenty-fifth hour
Of the day that started
On the footsteps of Eternity

HERENOW

No-Place

Sojourn in No-Place
In that perpetuity, there are some more days
They form the life remained only to live, and
A stream of all colors and nuances while
All dissolve in light. Arduously, I started to love
Writing with the color of Turquoise, a color
Thicker than the resin of the pines

There, which is, in fact, Here and Now
They threw me just as the wind
Scatters the flying seeds of
A Dandelion, so far. And, who knows
How many times, I fell to the ground of
Suffering or into the river of love, so
I may sail. A paper-boat, I am not!

Look, how the tears transform in emulsion
So that the Sun may burn them and make them
Nacre – that residue of pearls
Which is staunchly preserved in a plush box
Of mother's wedding-earrings

Well, I now uttered a word. May
It become a postcard I did not send
Accordingly, to an unknown recipient . . .

*The Utopian "No-Land", from the Persian eschatology, "Na Kooja Abad": No place, no land

Fahredin Shehu

The Dark Wind of the Universe

They used to count cities, decorated with
precious stones and temples which, today, we
discover. With nanotechnology-colors, they
painted millennials, prior to our understanding
that Love will pulsate like embers
of almost-burnt coals

The God is He Who Loves
regardless of how long he has travelled
from Here to Now
and regardless of how we have suffocated
in hatred and misfortune

The mystery, we may only reveal in the light
while we pale the waves of time

Today, with inspissated wishes, we
wave decades into the Loom of Life
while the Sun is growing older and is not adorned
as a deity, nor does the Moon evoke its fullness
while, sloppily, the dogs bark at her

That which luminates the organza of our memories
and, through them, changes nuances
with the jets of its hot rays, memoires – an oath
to the Universe that from one constellation to another
we shall travel and return where we were blown
by the dark wind of the distant skies

A Return

Full mouths
Empty pockets
So much hate here

I see Men dying
And the entire Shah Nameh of Firdousi
Condensed in the sky

I see the light of Men
In the darkest corners
of their being
and tears of their mothers
and rosaries to praise God
the god of ignorant and blind believers

Someone brought a golden box
Belgian Truffles and salty
Zoete Drops from Holland
With licorice flavor

I was absent at the time
I returned to mortify the fear

Encumbrance

Boughs
heavy with juicy fruits
my thirst and glutton
obedient under that image

All those who enter in
The dark homes, as dark as black
holes emanating a spectrum

And I see that fine light
white as my body
neon-white
independent from food and fruits
filled only with saturated visions
like blessings that exhaust
a tormented heart

HERENOW

Beyond the Calendar-Fast

Not a single stain
Smeared the light feathers
Of swans while they
Enjoyed a sunny afternoon

August, in its splendor, warms
the bones of the senile and boils
seeds of young plankton
on the surface of the human Soul

I run and run and run
I fell, I fall and I still shall fall
until my bruise bursts out the blood
and I shall wait seven days
for my bruise to turn yellow

I heal my wounds
lick them like a Lion
turn toward the sun to burn them
I fast in order to strengthen

Fahredin Shehu

When the Night Arrives . . .

The tunic of the sky is torn
and the light night is heavily
sprinkled with stardust

This is as I dream the dream
of the prophets from the past ages
remnants of todays
attempts of the malfeasant

The library of my being is opening
unfolding like the prayer-flags
of the far-away Nepal
minerals, plants, insects, animals
of all sorts; insects and
visible, semi-visible and invisible pluralities
multitudes are unifying in a procession an hour after
dawn when pomegranate-ous seeds of blood
transform into the colors of ruby and nacre

Let us all sing and celebrate life

The night has come

HERENOW

A Turquoise Ink for Spiritual Letters

I preserve a turquoise ink
to write only about love
and a blood-letter of inheritance, I keep
in a box inside an ox-tree
a copper plate for the lid
and a spout for heavy liqueur

My epitaph is sprinkled with Moschus
and it is made with light letters
of engraved Graphene. In green laser, it reads:
"Herein lies the soul of the light-man and
herein flow the remnants of another Aeon."

Amid the Urban Desert

Her bag is made of
Ostrich-leather, keeps all
Paraphernalia for a lusty ritual

Arranged dreams, she keeps folded in a roll
Hopes, like fireflies in a dark July-night
Form an aura or something like
A lightning-cloud above the head
Of the contemporary Eremite
Who walks amid the urban desert

A sonoric contamination
Ears are extinguished
Silence, declared defeat

Faces from No-Land

Fahredin Shehu

HERENOW

That Strange Something . . .

Silence, firmed
distilled
frozen

Breeze and the Zephyr
are folding
and shaking
and drying the palm-leaves

Talcum, sprinkled all around
the odor of Iodine, dissolved
in a stench of pine-resin
turpentine, leaking throughout
a porcelain dale
trampled with the heavy feet
of clay soldiers

She sees the Light!
Am I that light
I ask the terrestrial
and celestial entities

Am I a broken glass-vase
for your amethyst roses?

Am I that strange "Something"
Unfairly called
Homo Lucis?

Fahredin Shehu

Yes!

I am that
which
I am!

HERENOW

The Turret

In that steeple which is built over
Many years while others, in vain, thought
and hoped for the other's death

I climb in my bones
like toward high stairways
in the Alexandrian library in the
year of 2005, two days after an earthquake
shook Cairo . . . exactly, after 12 years

She prayed in Arabic
a Princess of some Arabian tribe
from the South . . . in her late years

Years, years, years
who's counting the days now,
and how much she feared death?
As if life is rolled on a reel of gilded threads . . .

Fahredin Shehu

My Borough

I never realized in that borough
why Light throw me out to walk
with a heavy burden and heavyheartedly

surrounded by vineyards like an amphitheater
in the dark nights to re-echo the chants and the Zikr[1]
of Dervishes[2], church bells and Adhan[3]
throughout the day

after the sun ceased to be adorned as god
whereas Pagans dressed in lianas in the middle of the city
prayed to Dodoles[4] for the rain to fall incessantly
during the dry heat-summers

when talking about love
was gravely shameful
and epitaphs were decorated with the droppings
of doves and crows made you think
that from the graveyard
Jackson Pollock walked out

---

[1] Sufi meditation / remembrance of God's Names
[2] Sufi pious man
[3] The Muslim call to prayer
[4] Fairies of Slavic origin that bring the rain

HERENOW

The Abyss of a Surface

In vain, they struggled
walls and faces, they painted
and burdens, they carried – the burdens of self
of all forms and those who appear on
the mirror – to recognize your nightmares
of the hidden evil, and, were flabbergasted

A white lit candle
in a dark chamber . . . instead of frankincense, I
wished a Myrrh – for ten years, I burned and feared
Pneumonia while during winter, I
was wettened in the water

But the Mandaean, I am not!

I tried as a crafted Soffer
to write in calligraphy a Mezuzot
jauntily as if the Clergy-Nazism
would call me an Apostate
and by quietism, I have been tormented
even a seven syllable-a day, not to utter
any Monatomic gold by the anonymous
Alchemist from Vienna

I administered
ruefully observed the Women of Prizrenska Gora
how they whitened their faces with mercury and arsenic
just as you are about to believe that they started freezing

Fahredin Shehu

and those who walked barefoot on the myriads of broken
pieces, and, sparsely, dispersed glass, aiming
at their enlightenment

We, all those born in that year, are
sisters and brothers like the particles and waves of
sunrays that penetrate through the Abyss of a Surface

HERENOW

The Coffin of a Female Corpse

For many years, Auntie kept
the cerements and glass bottles of Moschus
a gift from a Hajji-father from over
twenty-some years ago

Women gathered, and I – a boy
curiously, observing
the murmuring of the khodja-lady
while she bathed her for the last time
sprinkling with essence
and enlacing her with cere-cloth

The coffin was previously well-washed
with lye, so the wood-coffin
would become yellow as rice in saffron

The Men-congregation heavyheartedly waited

These recollections are stronger
even from the first pleasure of the many attempts
to eject a jet of semen
in my eleven-and-a half-years

staunchly hiding that from mother, father, sister

only brother laughed noiselessly
every time, he saw my blushed face
he knew!

Fahredin Shehu

Uncle

A senile with the white cap
whiter than his moustache
kept wine in a linen cloth
as if it was honey or
drained cream

Grandsons, he fed and with his wife, he ate
shar-cheese and grape, some chops of dried meat
from the garret where they used to dry apples, figs,
spices and red-hot pepper

During the evenings, some brandy and sauerkraut
under the arbor with the outspread boughs, when
he got drunk, he disregarded everything
even a forthcoming war but still, he feared
for his grandchildren

Yet, something from within convinced him
that this too shall pass, and it really passed
with priceless damage . . .

In the garden, the peaches bloomed
the Iris threw off lilac petals
and the Cala lilies, sowed by his wife, they
reminded him of Sama
the Mawlawi Dervish-dance
and, of all the places, in Bosnia
why in Bosnia? . . . He never told us!

HERENOW

My Fateful White Maltese

We could go to Ulcinj
in Montenegro
and no further
to get the smell of Iodine and
pines and hear the murmurs of palm leaves
when the wind blew them up

Then, to Backi Petrovac in Vojvodina
with my uncle who traded cereals, goose lard,
feathers, honey and red-hot chili peppers

On my jubilance – a day before my birthday
I got a puppy. I think it was a white Maltese
whom the tempestuous war-wind would take away
with myriads of words, bought, written, painted and
drawn with ink, tears in gold, Lapis Lazuli and
saffron, dissolved in rosewater

Even in blood, I wrote a love-letter which never
reached her. That letter was smoked with the combined
essence of Acacia flowers and of honeysuckle

My Father

You never closed your eyes
there was no repentance until I did
extinguish the fire – the one that permanently
        burned your heart

The flame that scalded your being was
only a protuberance of my innocence

You understood it in moments of your burn-out
when you didn't ask for the icy piece of watermelon
        in the middle of winter in 2011

All that you've asked me was to sleep by your bed
so that you would feel my whiff which was
        extinguishing that fire

To feel my smell and conviction that I
forgave you, father, for the times when
I was heedlessly wriggling in
        the Temple of Abraham

A Love-Path to Immortality

Those knowledge-givers
      with Nimbus
      looked at me
      with reverence

The green tears from red eyes, I
had never expected

My gowns of sky-color
Gave out the scent of white roses

Upon my entrance to that path, they
welcomed me, and said:
"Welcome to immortality!"

Fahredin Shehu

An Emerald Dane

On an emerald dane, I climbed
    full of breath
    full of self

Under the heavy-cold shadow
    of an Ash-tree, I took
    a rest for a while

A chrysoprase-epitaph
was observing me appallingly
crossly, and somberly, said:
"You, who in the world realized
That there is no East and there is no West
Since your world is round.
You, who said, so melt in Love
For eternity and a day more.
You, who discovered the secret in the light
While in grey nights, the Moon-walkers
Prayed to God:
See that then-ness and this now-ness
Are condensing with their naked bodies
In a solely single-being while you still
Recall when Time was a God."

HERENOW

I . . .

They denominated me as the Oscillator of knowledge
While I realized the pain by content and its attributes

You have counted nine layers of fog and you have
Never realized for whom

For far too long, you glared at refusals of heavy
Rebuke, a thunder-bolted reprimand
which burned a vowed-time of life

Fahredin Shehu

HE, Who Is Busy with Love . . .

With each swoon, I revealed a new world
On those returns, my eternal quietude
Was more and more quenched

While they were competing in offense,
Hatred and in "who's gonna win
In that Heaven and Hell", I paced
In the blink of an eye, and even
With the right one. While
Their God was punishing
Mine was busy making Love

HERENOW

Listen, O Life!

Throughout the world, I have paced like
the bread-giving wheat-cob,
      bowed, while the wind shook and bent
      an ell below my humbleness

Long ago, when I had been standing drowsily
with my light-year's reticent, thunder-like echo
      in emptied bones, I heard
      the Medullary of the straight-spine
      while it returned to Earth and I
      heard her, imbibed, she was thirsty

Listen to my life, oh all-blissful Light!
Just like God heard the progeny of Ishmael, listen
to our prayers while you hive

Fahredin Shehu

Faces from No-Place

So, with this breath-filled urn
and from Earth, she asked of
men with faces of No-Land

Limbs and bones shall dissolve
with the saffron color and the nard-fragrance
Iesha is waiting for me to fall down on his feet

My letters are round
their sounds are penetrating the being
in order to unify as river does with the ocean

*From the Persian eschatology, "Na Kooja Abad": No place, no land

The Weight of Pain

Fahredin Shehu

HERENOW

I.

With the harsh passage

of time, memories, bell-like

talk to me.

Bones have leaked

my Medullary. Who cares

that I have children . . .

II.

While my hair turns grey

from the purity of the Soul

my body is worn-out

from unstoppable questions

Am I, or not . . .

an Eremite?

III.

The tongue is knotted in nine

knots while I utter

that beautiful name

My God has mercy

for the burden of this Love

IV.

And . . .

the Heaven's gates

are opened to hear

that I knoweth the Pain

in its ponderosity and

grandeur

V.

Young saplings

the last moistening of dry plums

stars are dancing

in circles

We call this opacity

Love!

VI.

A warm touch

enkindles my skin

Whenever with every

alcove of my being

I want to live longer

all of a sudden, someone dies

VII.

In the flames of all colors, the

ground beneath my feet

is slippery. Ruthlessly, I

wanted to give another name

to beauty.

It is all in vain.

VIII.

A piece of my I-ness

I left in my dream

since in here

I did not tailor

any other vesture

this summer

IX.

In a multi-colored shell

two blue-nesses of a great ocean

are melted.

I peter out at this age

in a blue flame of Love.

X.

A huffish green, almost indigo

in potency, speaks to me

mannish-ly

about some baronial world

while I drink a green liqueur

of the Earth

XI.

I was told that it is much easier

to feed a blue whale

with fishes than to

obey the thirst

of the one in Love

eternally.

Fahredin Shehu

Innocent
Acts of
Consciousness

Fahredin Shehu

So Be It!

A vowel
then, another
a week of sorrow
simply, crying
a betrayal of manhood
a drop of curse
like this which was called here
at that mid-night
only the ray could
pass and trigger
a spectrum behind itself
jellied between the
infra and ultra-sounds
focused on the "I"
whom I have undressed
like layers of an onion
the eyes of the others were
burning and watering

London is calling but
here, as the invisible plurality, I am

So be it!

After the Flood

A lost child
we are all crying in front
of the TV screen. 20 years
after the war, she appears
but the mother is missing

all pushed to the wall
we who understood the pain
by colors
quantity
burden

Tamara asks for a new Synth
Reis, for SPS 4
Naside asks me
a husband who cares
about everyone
because all love him

I was absent for a moment
or a mere wanderer
between two
and / or
more worlds
named
semi-named
and unnamed

HERENOW

while I was knitting
a basket to catch the spawn
of evanished finbacks
at the time of the great
flood that which
cursed November
before the sunset

today is the same
the muezzin's call to prayer
is heard. I fear
the absence of the Sun
and the sunrays that
luminate my path
to the No-Place!

Fahredin Shehu

A Years-Collector

Often, I want to blow on
dried dandelions, and
from the bark of the willow, as I
used to do, to make a pan flute
to sing along
by the streamlet
that transports
particles of melted
souls and spirits
suffocated by Rusalkas[5]
while they drift to the Aegean Sea
and where they mix with
the sand on the bottom

Inside a copper, tiny cup
I keep rosewater which
long time ago had perfumed

Everything from my memories
could resurrect in
an innocent act of consciousness

Once again, in sheafs
I collect years
innocently, restlessly

---

[5] A fairy of Slavic origin who torments the souls of drowned people

HERENOW

as I sometimes
collected days
and months
under the shade
of a walnut tree
having a mouthful
of grapes

Fahredin Shehu

My Grandmother

She always asked for a pitcher
of ice-cold water, and frequently
gave me a tablecloth so I may collect
almost ripened Mulberries in uncle's garden
before they fell by themselves to the ground
and gathered gnats in flocks

She used to read Evrad[6] and Ya'sin[7]
every morning before the morning prayer
before she swallowed grains of frankincense
and two spoons of honey, in particular
the one from the meadows of Deçan[8]

The world knows two world wars
I also know two plus
The death of a grandmother who made
out of me a yokemate in suffer of
giants and pivots of misfortune

---

[6] Prayers formulated by the Sufis that are given to the chosen
[7] The Sura from The Holy Qur'an that is considered as the heart of the holy book of Islam
[8] A city in Southwest-Kosovo

I Fear Not!

Late snow fell on
        Peach-flowers
what a strange season
        we live in
no other time can I recall
        when I had
        been trying
        to remain
        so intensely
        alert

While the sky is preparing
        to build different and
        always-changing
        sculptures of clouds
something will fall
apart from ice and liquids

Something strange sowed fear
        what may be
        more terrible than death?

        I fear not!

Fahredin Shehu

The Blooming Acacia

I was taught about Pan in school
and about Arrabal[9], 30 years later

About Attar, I was taught by my grandmother
without her mentioning it, until I found *Pend- Nameh*[10]
a translation by some Bosnian Sage

And again – after some
20 years passed; there, between their
thighs, I was serene

Neither Pan had anything to do with
my pan-icking
nor Attar, with my misfortune
to become a healer of work-worn bodies
and spooky souls that pace
with heavy lungs toward the hill
of flourished Acacias
in early Spring

---

[9] Fernando Arrabal, a Surrealist, was, together with Alejandro Jodorowsky, the founder of the Panic Movement.
[10] The book of advice by the Persian Sufi master, Feriduddin Attar

The Mirror

Pearls that are not worn
on the neck of the Beauty do not grow
and do not keep their warmth or weight

And the petals not kissed
languish and change their color

The Soul without love
dries like the saliva of a female
spider who in order to give birth
must eat the male

And I, shall today, drink
the color of Malachite
until it becomes transparent
like mere glass or a mirror
so that there may be seen
thousands of "I"

Fahredin Shehu

Come on!

That solidified heart
that pure, dark, luminous,
firm Onyx

That fat sadness
And in layers-layered
suffering

This handful of
wishes-misleading set-ups
shamed, the pride

And my exclamation
"Come on!"
reveals a secret
yet it hides
either in light
or in its lack of action

A Drop of Happiness

Beyond white clouds, there was
a chill. Yet, the happiness is paid off
while the invisible plurality took away
the breath from the lungs
and, along with the breath, one's sanity

We ceased to believe
those long stories and salty words

Really,
God never
rolled a dice!

Fahredin Shehu

On Sound, Secrets, Love and Travesty

A soft sound
presses on my diaphragm
and squeezes my ear's membrane

The Sun burned all pellicles
when loners were praying
in the dark and gazing at the
kindled candle-flame

The man, fed throughout many years
with compost of nettle leaves
in order to achieve enlightenment
for redemption for the sins committed
ordered by the tormented mother
that is a real sin
a great sin, yes!
to kill through pishogue
his spiteful uncle

Milarepa, for God's sake
why did you not come when
anguish conquered you and
the world pissed you off
to drink with me a cup of wine
blended with a little patience
and enlightened with love?

HERENOW

Since God is only
the one Who loves, and
everything else
is just a farce!

A Love-Song

Oh

Forgetfulness,

Where are you?

HERENOW

That Wine . . .

That wine we have promised
to drink on the day of
our wedding – it happened
some years ago, and that
promise to go to the shore
and observe the seagulls bringing
fishes and throwing bones . . .

Rosemary, in bloom

Summer is different here
on the seaside – even the songs
have another tune and the words
different vowels and syllables . . .

Wet feet stepping on the Laguna
of dry, tiny pearls – in our
passion for living, death
seems as just a play

When the curtain closes, end
all masquerades

Fahredin Shehu

Epilogue

Photo by Rromir Imami

about the Author...

Fahredin Shehu is a writer, a critic, Independent Scientific Researcher in the fields of World Spiritual Heritage and Sacral Esthetics and a certified expert in Adult learning on the platforms of Capacity Building, Training, Coaching, Mentoring and Facilitating. A member of the European Academy of Poets and the Poetry Center at Roehampton University in London, Shehu is Director and Organizer of the Kosova International Poetry Festival.

Born in 1972 in Rahovec – South-East of Kosova, Shehu graduated from Prishtina University with a degree in Oriental Studies. Passionate about Calligraphy, he actively works on discovering new mediums and techniques for this specific form of plastic art.

Fahredin Shehu has several books in Albanian and English. *The Pen* – selected poetry in Serbian was published in 2013 by Archipelago Press in Belgrade, Serbia. His literary works in English include the following: *Dismantling Hate*, an E-Book, published in 2010 by Ronin Press in London;

Crystalline Echoes, hard copy and E-Book, published in 2011 by Corpus Editora in Porto, Portugal, *Pleroma's Dew*, hard copy and Kindle / Amazon Edition, published in 2012 by Inner Child Press International in State College, USA; *The Honeycomb*, authors edition, published in 2013 is structured through eight angels in eight human occupations as an accomplishment of Bee Honeycomb. The reader is, then, made into the ninth angel in a symbolism of Enneagram, an approach that is the first in Albanian.

Furthermore, the author's published works include *MAELSTROM. The Four Scrolls of an Illyrian Sage*, an epic poem in English, published in 2014 by Inner Child Press International in State College, USA; *Bonds*, hard copy and Kindle / Amazon Edition, published in 2016 by Inner Child Press International in State College, USA; *Elisir* (a critically acclaimed work that was printed with the title *Elixir* in its bilingual edition – in Albanian and Italian, published in 2017 by Pelicano Libri in Rome, Italy and *Neon Child*, hard copy and Kindle / Amazon Edition, published in 2018 by Inner Child Press International in State College, USA.

In his *MAELSTROM*, Shehu offers spiritual insights, visions, a creative turmoil in mental faculties of the creator that oscillates between Theurgy and Revelation. This epic poem displays a spatio-temporal efficiency of poetry as the best tool for telling the untold. As for his book of poetry, *Bonds*, the author was nominated for the 2018 Pulitzer Prize for Letters.

Fahredin Shehu's literary creations have been translated into numerous languages, including English, French, Italian, Spanish, Polish, Greek, Serbian, Croatian, Bosnian, Macedonian, Roma, Swedish, Turkish, Arabic, Hebrew, Romanian, Chinese, Maltese, Bahasa / Malaysian, Benghali, Frisian and Sicilian.

The author is an accomplished editor as well, as his following editorial contributions demonstrate: *The Anthology of Kosovo Contemporary Poetry in Turkish*; *The Balkan Anthology*, an extensive anthological compilation of contemporary Pan-Balkan poetry, published in 2018 by Inner Child Press International in State College, USA; an anthology on the paintings of Hiernoimus Bosch and Peter Breugel; an anthology of poems by W. H. Auden, William Carlos Williams, Sylvia Plath,

Anne Sexton, Czeslaw Milosz, John Berryman, Billy Collins, Charles Simic, et al., together with the newly-minted poems, written especially for this collection, by Rae Armantrout, Peg Boyers, Robert Fanning, Alfred Corn, Ravi Shankar, Kaveh Akbar, Kimiko Hahn, et al. – with an introduction by the noted art historian Margaret A. Sullivan and her poet son, David Allen Sullivan.

For his role in bridging nations, Fahredin Shehu has been acknowledged as the 2014 Poet Laureate of the Gold Medal for Poetry by Axlepin Publishing in The Philippines. He was selected for this award from among many globally recognized writers, photographers and painters, all of who had contributed to the betterment of humanity. Other awards through which the author has been singled out include the Naji Nahman Prize for Poetry in 2016 (Beirut, Lebanon) and the Veilero Prize for Poetry in 2017 (Rome, Italy).

Contributions to Anthologies, Yearbooks & Journals

~ *The World Poets Yearbook* 2009, Bei Jing, China

~ *Poetas del Mundo Anthology*, Santiaogo de Chile

~ *Blue Max Magazine*, Dublin, Ireland

~ *Check Point Poetry*, Le Reti di Dedalus, Italy,

~ *The Alquimia de la Terra Anthology*, Universidad da Huelva, Spain

~ *Ann Arbour Review*, Michigan, USA

~ *Coldnoon Literary Magazine*, Jawhalal Nehru University, New Delhi, India

~ *World Healing World Peace*, international poetry anthology, Inner Child Press International, State College, USA

~ *Anthology for the Rights of Hazara People*, Oslo, Norway

What Others Are Saying

In Fahredin Shehu's poetry, I find a rare combination of passion and compassion. He is a learned poet who knows that true creativity in art is to know the traditions – his own first, and then the other important traditions. This creative poet, then, adds something new into the traditions, something that was not there before his poems were created.

This is how I met the Kosovar poet Fahredin Shehu both, as a person who became my friend and through his poetry, which has developed into something very important during the last few years. Empathy is a word which I like to use when describing his poetry. Here, we find a closeness to Earth and the body; we find not only sensibility but also brilliant expressions of a man's lust. All of this is combined with an awareness of the sacred. He is learned in symbolism and mythology, both from the Islamic and Christian traditions, but also from the rich folklore of his native part of Europe and of regions beyond. He can be direct, he can be overwhelming, but first and foremost, he expresses a sincere belief in poetry as a power to heal wounded souls and to show us something more important than greed and wealth. We read about East and West, here are also the North and the South. But the poet knows and tells us that whatever and wherever the place is on our small planet, people are very much alike – when seen from the perspective of the Universe. There is happiness and hope in these poems, written by a poet from a small country where people have been suffering for decades from wars and suppression.

Knut Ødegård
Poet
Norway

When a poet with a vast horizon such as Fahredin Shehu says *HERENOW*, I embrace the challenging adventures of a tour open to every possible 'herenow' of every possible subject. I keep enjoying the enriching ride.

Tarık Günersel
Poet
Turkey

Some poetry collections work on the emotions, some work on the intellect – *HERENOW* works on all levels to beguile. These are poems that are deeply felt with something spiritual infusing them all. Spiritual not religious, though the poems often find a wellspring in Sufi approaches to Islam which underlines the journeys made, the reaching out from the personal, the familial to the universal. There is an immediacy here; the poems are sensual with a smell, taste, sound, touch taking you to the heart of being there. There are also fierce and angry poems that rail at injustice and offer love instead. One poem, "Toward Hope", might well have been the title of the collection – "Say a word, oh poet / the word as rocket to hit / the hearts made of stone". *HERENOW* is such a rocket.

Professor Patrick Lodge
Retired
Ireland / Wales

Stop worshipping Time, as Time is God no more. Distant Earths rotate, but for you there is no East or West. To be Here, to be Now, to bark like a dog, to be sonorous like the sky. There, you find yourself resembling nobody and name your self Fahredin Shehu. The last angel of love on Earth, or trying to be one.

Professor Keijiro Sugo
Meiji University
Japan

Fahredin Shehu is a writer of expansive lyric gifts, vision and daring. His poems evoke possible worlds and worlds that are impossible, as well as finding revelations in the everyday. He is a writer to feast on, as inspiring in celebration as he is insightful in elegy.

Professor Fiona Sampson
Roehampton University
UK

a few words from the Publisher . . .

I first met Fahredin Shehu in September of 2015 at the inaugural Kosovo International Poetry Festival. I have known him through cyberspace since 2011 when we at Inner Child Press, now Inner Child Press International launched our first initiative of the anthology *World Healing, World Peace*.

Meeting Mr. Shehu, whom I now embrace as my brother was a very rewarding experience in spite of my awe-struck consciousness of participating in my very first International Poetry Festival. I have since went on to be a part of, as well as being a key note speaker and lecturer at many other subsequent events to include Morocco, Tunisia, Macedonia, Jordan, Palestine, to name a few. Because of Fahredin's catalystic-ism, my personal poetic life has been greatly enhanced . . . but this is not about me, though it may appear so.

Mr. Shehu has that particular type of empowering, insightful and learned spirit that affects the unassuming and the "aware" in a very profound way. I once told my beloved hülya, that Fahredin is the type of soul at whose feet I could sit and listen as well as probe the depths of his knowledge and be quite content. I too am a lover of knowledge. In his conversations, this book and all of his previous writings, if you listen carefully to the voice of his evocations and sharing, there is a fruit – sometimes hidden and some times obvious. For myself, it is a divinely sweet fare that I always look forward to ingesting and hopefully digesting to add to the girth of my consciousness as I seek to expand. His poetry makes it that much more palatable.

In conclusion, all I can say is that I hope you find the work of Mr. Shehu, a.k.a. Fahredin, my brother, rewarding for your soul, your consciousness and the journey you are on.

Bless Up

Bill

Chairperson
Inner Child Press International

Inner Child Press

Inner Child Press is a Publishing Company Founded and Operated by Writers. Our personal publishing experiences provides us an intimate understanding of the sometimes-daunting challenges Writers, New and Seasoned may face in the Business of Publishing and Marketing their Creative "Written Work".

For more Information

Inner Child Press

www.innerchildpress.com

intouch@innerchildpress.com

www.ingramcontent.com/pod-product-compliance
Lightning Source LLC
LaVergne TN
LVHW051843080426
835512LV00018B/3046